Also by Raejean Kanter:

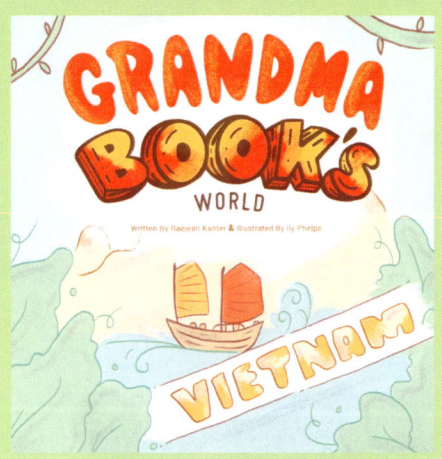  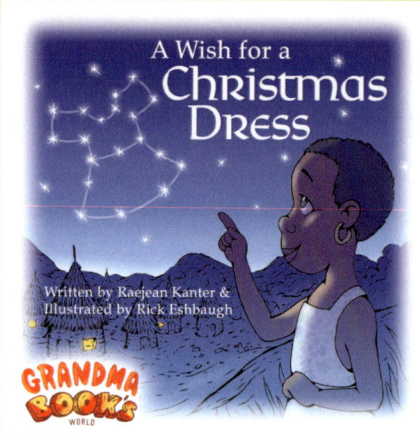

Meet the author at: www.grandmabookworld.com
Facebook: @grandmabooksworld

Published by Orange Hat Publishing 2020
ISBN 978-1-64538-112-9
Library of Congress Control Number: 2020900865

Copyrighted © 2020 by Raejean Kanter
All Rights Reserved
Two Countries, Three Friends
Written by Raejean Kanter
Illustrated by Rick Eshbaugh

All Rights Reserved. Written permission must be secured from the publisher to use or reproduce any part of this book, except for brief quotations in critical reviews or articles.

For information, please contact:
Orange Hat Publishing
www.orangehatpublishing.com
414.212.5477

This book is dedicated to
Jill and Kumar Kolin
and
Jim and Molly Kanter
For raising their children to become
loving, caring and gentle global citizens

Written by Raejean Kanter
In collaboration with
Nikhil Kolin and Jacob Kolin
Illustrated by Rick Eshbaugh

One day when Grandma Book was visiting her two grandsons, Nikhil and Jacob, they told her that they had an idea for a book they would like her to write.

They said the name of the book would be **Two Countries, Three Friends**.

Grandma Book was interested in hearing about their idea.

She asked them to tell her more about it.

Nikhil started the story with a question.
"You know our friend Lorenzo, right?" he asked her.
"Do you remember that he lives in Italy?"

She said that she did remember that was where he lived.

"Well," he continued, "we live in the United States, and even though we don't live in the same country, we are friends."

Jacob continued, "We think it would be great for kids to know that you can have friends in other countries around the world."

"That sounds like a very good idea to me. Let's talk more about it. Let's start with how you met Lorenzo," said Grandma Book.

LORENZO

That's easy! Our mom and Lorenzo's mom, Zoe, were friends when they were in college. One day Mom told us that she and her family were coming to visit us.

"They live in Italy and will be staying with us for a week. There is a boy in the family named Lorenzo who is about your age."

We had a lot of questions about him.

Did he speak English?

Did he like to build with Legos?

Did he like to be silly like we do?

Mom said we would find out all the answers to those questions when we met him.

The next few days were really fun.

We went to the park to climb, slide, and swing.

Soon our whole family was on a large plane flying over the Atlantic Ocean. It took a long time, and we both fell sleep.

Mom woke us up and said we would soon be landing in Italy.

When the plane landed, there was Lorenzo!

We were so happy to see each other that we all started to jump up and down.

Lorenzo lives in the northern part of Italy near the mountains called the Alps.

It was very beautiful.

As we began exploring, we learned that many things were the same and some were a bit different.

Some people spoke English, but more spoke Italian. They had pizza, but it didn't taste the same. There were television shows, but not the same ones we had at home. And when you said "ciao" it could mean either hello or goodbye.

There were also many people sailing and swimming.

That looked like fun.

Others were climbing the mountains. Maybe we will try that when we get older.

The next day, we all went on a road trip to Venice. Venice is really a different kind place. There are no roads for cars to drive on. Instead there are canals for boats.

We took a ride in a special kind of boat called a gondola. The person who steers it stands and sings at the same time.

Then we noticed the stores had windows with many kinds of things to see in them.

There were masks, toys, and things made of bright-colored glass.

We went into the store to pick out one thing to buy. It was a hard choice.

Before leaving Venice, we had a special treat to eat.
It was GELATO! It is like ice cream but much better,
and there are so very many flavors.

When we returned to Lorenzo's house, Mom said that it was time to pack up to go home.

We were sad because we knew we would miss our friend Lorenzo again. He said he would miss us also.

It was fun visiting our friend and learning about Italy.

"Well, Grandma Book, that's the story," said Nikhil.
"Do you think you can write it?" asked Jacob.

About the Collaborators

You may have noticed in the credits of this book that I had two collaborators in writing it. They are Nikhil and Jacob Kolin, the two youngest of my six grandchildren. One day when I was visiting them, they told me that they had an idea about a book they thought I should write. With that, the process you have read about began. They were consulted along the way and made some changes they thought would make the book better. It was a joy watching them use their creative minds to write a book of which we can all be proud.

One of their favorite hobbies is creating their own books. They enjoy working together to tell many tales. It wouldn't surprise me if one day you will be reading a book authored by both of them.

My advice to grandparents is to enter into a project like this with your grandchildren. I learned so much about them, and hope that I have left them with an experience they won't forget.

About Us

Raejean Kanter
Author

Rick Eshbaugh
Illustrator

&

In her series **Grandma Book's World**, Raejean Kanter combines two of her passions: love of children and travel. A grandmother of six, she has traveled to over fifty countries in the world. The mission of the series is to help young children learn about other cultures to foster a greater understanding of inclusion. Ms. Kanter has a BBA from St. Norbert College and a MEd from Cardinal Stritch University.

Rick Eshbaugh has been an animator and graphic designer in southeastern Wisconsin for over thirty years. Recently retired, he has returned to his early interest in children's book illustration. He enjoyed his first two assignments, collaborating with Ms. Kanter on *Some Call Me Santa* and *A Wish for a Christmas Dress*. *Two Countries, Three Friends* promotes friendship around the world, an effort to which Rick is proud to contribute.

www.ingramcontent.com/pod-product-compliance
Lightning Source LLC
LaVergne TN
LVRC090218080426
835507LV00038B/149